Gioachino ROSSINI

GUILLAUME TELL
OVERTURE

Edited by
Clark McAlister

Study Score
Partitur

SERENISSIMA MUSIC, INC.

PREFACE

To be as popular as they are, the overtures to Rossini's operas have been treated very poorly by publishers, both Italian and foreign, throughout most of their histories. Even the most recent editions, as thorough as many of them are, do not answer all of the questions concerning textual matters.

It will probably always be so. First, many of the textual inconsistencies one finds come from Rossini's own manuscripts. During most of his career, Rossini was working at an incredibly fast and furious pace, so it is not surprising that some relatively small details would escape his attention. Also, working at such speed inevitably took a toll on the legibility of some of his manuscripts, thereby adding another layer of potential uncertainty. While the context will frequently clarify such matters, in numerous cases different readings are possible.

Second, these scores come from a time when performance practices still assumed that the written score would be modified in performance in certain fairly predictable ways. Broadly speaking, for example, a certain lightness of execution was expected, the notation of which in our own era requires a rather liberal use of staccato dots. In Rossini's time, this refinement of notation was not practiced.

Third, in the case of works written for the stage which were already frequently performed during the composer's lifetime, it is quite logical to believe that Rossini's manuscript scores represent only an intermediate stage in the perfection of his music. The world of opera, more than that of concert music, thrives on revisions and alterations. Many of these changes, of course, are made to suit specific circumstances, and the composer would not want them to become permanent. Norman Del Mar, in his invaluable book *Orchestra Variations*, points out that, on the other hand, some of these changes represent composer-sanctioned second thoughts and even, sometimes, improvements over the original version of the text to be found in the manuscript score. As Del Mar says, "Not all traditions are bad and many derive from the composer himself or the society to which he belonged."

The question, then, becomes how to distinguish one kind of change from the other—when a later source differs from an earlier one, which reading should be followed? If we accept that in many instances no definitive answer is possible, we must follow our best understanding of Rossini's style, both as an individual composer and as one working contentedly within the prevailing performance practices of his time. The present editions of these overtures seek to do just that—by examining as many sources as possible, to arrive at performing texts which both reflect the spirit of the composer and are as practical as possible for the use of modern orchestras.

There is one aspect of this and other scores of Rossini's that needs more clarification than will fit practically in the space of a footnote. One of Rossini's favorite string colors is the rhythmic tapping, or clicking, of the bow against the string, indicated by the instruction **battute**, or "beaten." Some writers (including Christine Amner in *The A to Z of Foreign Musical Terms* and Walter Kolneder in *Auffürungspraxis bei Vivaldi*) feel that this instruction at least implies execution by using the wood of the bow, col legno. But Norman Del Mar, in *A Companion to the Orchestra*, suggests otherwise. In his discussion of the term col legno he writes:

> It is true that if executed honestly with only the wood of the bow very little actual note is heard, and when composers write important note formations col legno, such Berlioz in the Witches' Sabbath movement of *Symphonie fantastique*, the players will generally cheat by turning the bows sideways to that a little of the hair also comes into play. If they cheat too much, only the hair being brought into contact with the strings, this creates a quite different device, which is found constantly in Rossini under the term battute. . . . None of these vertical techniques produces any enormous volume, especially in view of the cautious attitude of the musicians . . .

To this discussion, three further considerations may be added. First, it will be seen that this technique also yields a staccato "sound," so that the use of staccato dots in notating its use is unnecessary. Second, there are passages which lend themselves to this style of playing but for which Rossini did not indicate battute. When, in these editions, the editor suggests the use of this technique the term [battute] will appear, but the composer's staccato indications will be retained. Finally, Rossini is sometimes not clear about when players should return from battute to conventional arco, whether staccato or not. Although the context may seem to make these changeover points evident, in these editions battute will always be "cancelled" by the term arco.

I wish to thank Nancy M. Bradburd of the Philadelphia Orchestra and Clinton F. Nieweg, Librarian (retired) of that Orchestra, for their insights and suggestions during the preparation of these editions. I am most fortunate to be able to partake of their vast experience in these matters.

The Editor
Spring 2014

The opera *Guillaume Tell* was first performed at the Théâtre de l'Académie Royale de Musique in Paris on August 3rd, 1829. The cello section of that orchestra comprised ten players, and Rossini's scoring of the opening section of the Overture was written to account for all ten players—five soli and five ripieni players, the latter divided as two plus three. Many orchestras today do not have so many players in their cello section, and therefore in this edition the cello ripieni parts in mm. 1-48 are cued into the double bass part. However, these cues are written to sound at cello pitch--that is, they are written an octave higher in the double bass part than the passages appear in the cello part, because it is quite clear that these parts are intended to sound in the cello octave, not an octave lower.

Available evidence suggests that in the first production the two trumpet parts were doubled between mm. 226-477 of the Overture. Among other considerations, the concertmaster's part in the original material, which is a kind of short score, mentions four trumpets. (Existing material from the first performances also suggests that four extra horns were engaged.)

ORCHESTRA

2 Flutes

Piccolo

2 Oboes (one doubling English Horn)

2 Clarinets

2 Bassoons

4 Horns

2 Trumpets

3 Trombones

Timpani

Percussion (Triangle, Cymbals, Bass Drum)

Strings

Duration: ca.11-12 minutes
Premiere: August 3, 1829
Paris, Théâtre de l'Académie Royale de Musique
Soli, Chorus and Orchestra, Henri Valentino (conductor)

© Copyright 2014 Clark McAlister.
All rights reserved.
This study score is an unabridged reprint – in reduced format – of the
large conductor's score first issued by Kalmus as A8984. The large score and
orchestra parts are also available for sale from Serenissima Music, Inc.

GUILLAUME TELL
Overture

GIOACHINO ROSSINI
Performing Edition by Clark McAlister

* In mm.1-48, the bottom two lines of the Violoncello part are cued into the Double Bass part.

SERENISSIMA MUSIC, INC.

* Clarinets, m. 143 – Some sources show a written G rather than B flat.
** Clarinets, m. 147 – Some sources show a written D rather than F sharp.

33

* In some sources, the Flute and Piccolo appear an octave higher in mm. 421-422.

www.ingramcontent.com/pod-product-compliance
Lightning Source LLC
Chambersburg PA
CBHW081329040426
42453CB00013B/2346